THE
SUN

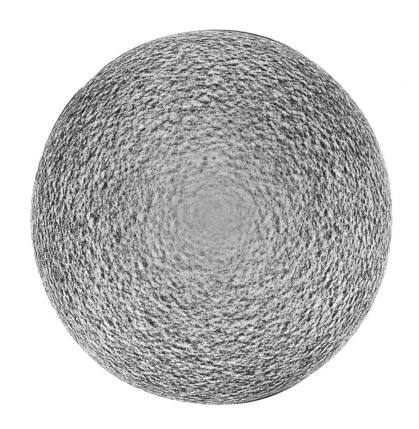

TIM FURNISS

RAINTREE
STECK-VAUGHN
PUBLISHERS

A Harcourt Company

Austin   New York
www.steck-vaughn.com

spinning through space
THE
SUN

Titles in the series:

The Earth • The Moon • The Solar System

Cover photograph:
The spacecraft *Ulysses* traveled over the sun's poles in 1994–95 [inset left];
the spacecraft *SOHO* that stays in orbit around the sun [inset bottom];
the aurora borealis [inset middle]; the sun's violent surface [main].

Title page: The sun from *SOHO*, a spacecraft launched in 1996 to observe the sun.

Published by Raintree Steck-Vaughn Publishers, an imprint of Steck-Vaughn Company

Printed in Italy. Bound in the United States.
1 2 3 4 5 6 7 8 9 0 05 04 03 02 01

Library of Congress Cataloging-in-Publication Data
Furniss, Tim.
The sun / Tim Furniss.
    p.   cm.—(Spinning through space)
    Includes bibliographical references and index.
    Summary: Explains the composition and behavior of the sun, our nearest star.
    ISBN 0-7398-2739-1 (HC)
    0-7398-3091-0 (SC)
    1. Sun—Juvenile literature.
    [1. Sun.]
    I. Title. II. Series.
    QB521.5.F87   2000
    523.7—dc21   00-020758

CONTENTS

THE NEAREST STAR

The night sky twinkles with thousands of tiny lights. Some are very faint, and some are quite bright. On a clear night, when you look up into the sky, you are looking at about 5,000 stars.

During the day, the stars are still there, but only one star is bright enough to be seen. This star is our sun. It is about 93 million mi. (150 million km) away, which is about the perfect distance. If the sun were a bit closer, we would fry from the heat. If it were farther away, we would freeze.

If the sun were the size of a soccer ball, Earth would be a pea 98 ft (30 m) away.

The sun shining brightly in the Earth's sky ▶

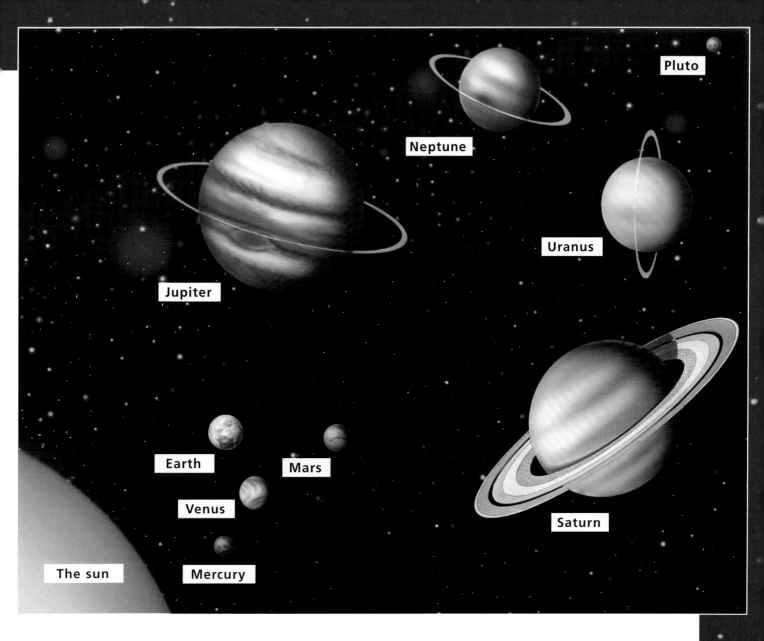

Pluto

Neptune

Uranus

Jupiter

Earth

Mars

Venus

Saturn

The sun

Mercury

▲ The solar system. The nine planets orbit the sun.

It takes light from the sun 8 minutes and 17 seconds to reach the Earth.

Our planet, Earth, is one of nine planets that orbit the sun. Mercury and Venus are the planets closest to the sun. Then come Earth, Mars, Jupiter, Saturn, Uranus, Neptune, and Pluto. Pluto, the smallest planet, is the farthest away from the sun, at a distance of 3.6 billion mi. (5.76 billion km). From Pluto, the sun would look like a small, bright star. Some planets have moons. The Earth has one moon. The sun and its nine planets and their moons are called the solar system.

THE TINY SUN

The sun and the stars that we can see are part of a galaxy. When you look into the night sky, you may be able to see part of our galaxy stretching above you like a faint band of clouds, filled with the lights of over 100 billion stars.

▼ The Milky Way, with the sun's position shown

We call this galaxy the Milky Way. The Milky Way is actually the outer arm of a spinning galaxy in space, called a spiral galaxy. From a distance, the Milky Way looks like the spiral made from fireworks.

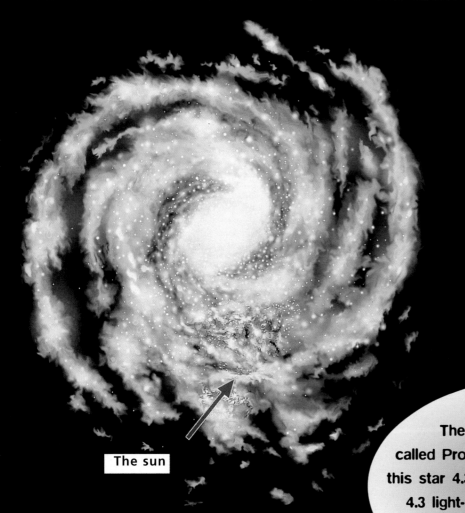

The sun

The nearest star to the sun is called Proxima Centauri. It takes light from this star 4.3 years to reach us. This is called 4.3 light-years. The sun is 270,000 times closer to us than Proxima Centauri.

It takes a rocket three days to fly to the moon. It would take a rocket 440 billion years to reach the nearest galaxy!

The sun is a very ordinary and small star compared with most of the stars in the Milky Way galaxy. The Milky Way is just one of millions of other galaxies in the vast universe. The sun's place in the universe is very small and insignificant, but for us it is a vital life source. Without the sun, our Earth would be a huge, dark, freezing lump of rock.

▼ The sun from the surface of Betelgeuse, a red giant star in the Orion constellation. It is 300 times larger than the sun. Its light takes 650 years to reach Earth.

SUN FACTS

The sun is on an outer arm of the Milky Way, about 32,000 light-years from the center of the galaxy. Although the sun is small compared with most of the stars in the universe, it looks big to us. And it is about 92 million mi. (150 million km) away!

The diameter of the sun around its equator is 864,972 mi. (1,392,000 km), compared with the Earth's 7,953-mi. (12,800-km) diameter. It is 330,000 times heavier than Earth. The sun contains 99.9 percent of the mass of the whole solar system.

The sun takes 225 million years to orbit the Milky Way galaxy. It travels at a speed of 1,336 mi. (2,150 km) per second.

▼ The burning sun sets over the Pacific Ocean.

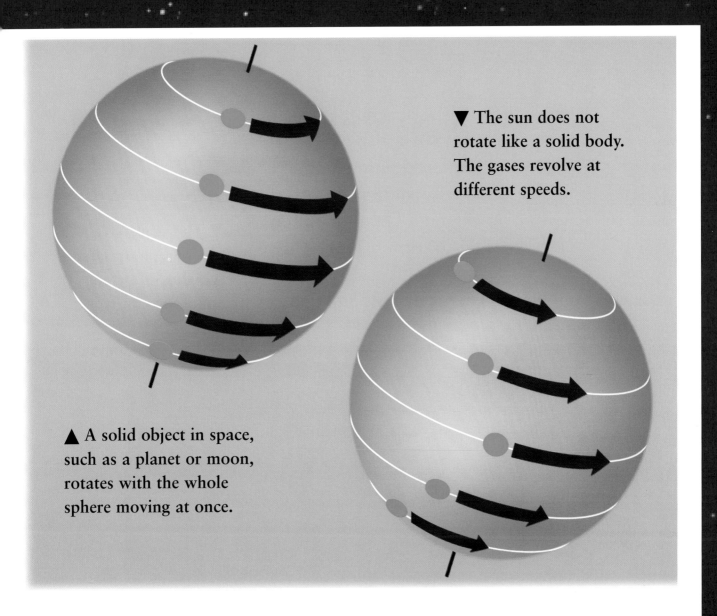

▼ The sun does not rotate like a solid body. The gases revolve at different speeds.

▲ A solid object in space, such as a planet or moon, rotates with the whole sphere moving at once.

The swirling sphere

Unlike Earth, which is a solid mass of rock, the sun is a swirling, seething sphere of hot gases. Different areas of the sun spin around at different speeds. The equatorial zones around the middle of the sun make a full turn in 25 days. The polar regions at the top and bottom of the sun spin around in 33 days.

The temperature at the center of the sun is 59 million° F (15 million° C). The surface is cooler at 10,830° F (6,000° C).

The fiery heart of the solar system

The sun produces most of the heat and energy in our solar system. The center of the sun is like a huge nuclear furnace. The temperature and pressure inside it are so high that they set off atomic reactions. Every second, 700 million tons of hydrogen fuse together to form helium. This process is called nuclear fusion. It releases enormous amounts of energy as heat and light.

The sun's mass amounts to 4.5 septillion tons.

▼ This is an X-ray photograph of the sun showing its violent atmosphere at work.

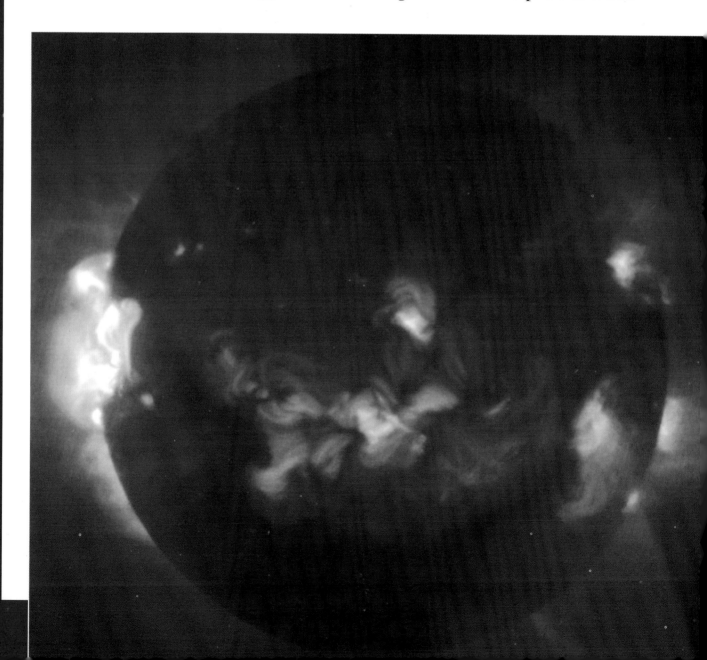

A star is formed out of a cloud of gas and dust. It begins to shine for millions of years before it swells up into a red giant and becomes a white dwarf star.

The dying sun

The sun's energy is slowly dying. It loses about 4 million tons of mass every second. That sounds like a lot, but it is really a very small amount compared with the sun's total mass. Millions of years in the future, the sun will run out of hydrogen. It will then expand and smother the whole solar system. Even then the sun will not be totally destroyed. It will cool down and become a tiny, weak star.

The sun uses 22 million tons of hydrogen each year. Scientists have calculated that the sun could go on shining for five billion years before it cools down.

THE SURFACE OF THE SUN

The sun is a life-giving furnace. It is an ocean of fire and flames. Energy produced at the core of the sun radiates out toward the surface.

Layer upon layer of hot gas

The surface of the sun is a seething mass of hydrogen gas, called the photosphere. The temperature ranges from 7,772° F (4,300° C) to 16,232° F (9,000° C). The photosphere provides most of the light that comes from the sun.

corona

energy radiating out

photosphere

core

chromosphere

◄ This cutaway diagram of the sun shows the different layers of the star.

The upper level of the photosphere is called the chromosphere. This is a stormy region of very hot gases, where, the temperature rises to 34 million °F (1 million °C). The chromosphere is about 9,942 mi (16,000 km) thick.

Above the chromosphere, the sun has a halo of even hotter gases called the corona. Some parts of the corona are 10 million °F (4 million °C). The outer layers of the corona are made up of hot gas blowing off from the sun. This streams away from the sun and is called the solar wind.

◄ Solar storms send atomic particles toward the Earth, causing the aurora borealis.

◀ A view of the sun from *Skylab 4* space station. This photo shows some of the most spectacular solar flares ever recorded.

Sunspots

The surface of the sun can sometimes erupt with flames as energy escapes from its core to burst up through a sunspot. Sunspots are the dark patches that can be seen on the photosphere. They are the sites of violent storms caused by disturbances that block the flow of energy from inside the sun. As a result, the bursts of hot energy cannot reach the surface, which then becomes colder and therefore less bright. Sunspots look almost black against the red-hot background of the sun.

Solar storms send out atomic particles that can destroy the Earth's ionosphere. These solar storms often cause radio interference and aurorae, red and green glowing lights in the night sky on Earth.

Sometimes, the sunspots release the energy. The result is sudden eruptions of gas that cause flares to shoot out from the sun's surface. These are called solar flares.

Sunspots and solar flares come in an 11-year cycle. For several years, there is a buildup of activity that reaches a peak, then becomes quiet again.

Prominences

Sometimes huge, almost frightening, flames spew from the sun. These are called prominences. The prominences spurt out, like huge fiery blasts, without warning. There is a sudden upward rush of energy from the sun.

▼ This ultraviolet image of the sun's surface shows how violent it really is.

THE SUN AND EARTH

The moving sun?

The sun appears to move across our sky—rising in the morning and setting at night. As the Earth moves around the sun, it is rotating or spinning around like a top. As the Earth spins toward the east, the sun in the sky appears to move upward. It crosses the sky, setting in the west in the evening. About midday, the sun is at its highest point in the sky.

The sun causes shadows. When the sun is low in the sky, it casts long shadows. As it slowly climbs, the shadows get smaller because it is shining almost directly downward. As the sun moves, so do the shadows.

▼ The setting sun photographed at six-minute intervals in midsummer

The Earth's axis is not perfectly upright as it orbits the sun. It is inclined at an angle of 23.5 degrees. This tilt causes the seasons.

The seasons

Parts of the Earth close to the North and South poles do not receive sunlight during some weeks of the winter in the Northern and Southern hemispheres.

The tilting of the Earth causes the seasons. In the winter, the sun seems to be lower in the sky and does not shine very long each day. This is because the Earth is tilted away from the sun. It is colder. During the summer, the Earth is tilted toward the sun, so it is higher in the sky and stays for longer. Then it is hotter.

Not all parts of the Earth are at the same distance from the sun at the same time. So when it is winter in the Northern Hemisphere, it is summer in the Southern Hemisphere, depending on which area is tilted toward the sun.

▼ This artwork shows how the Earth's tilt causes the four seasons.

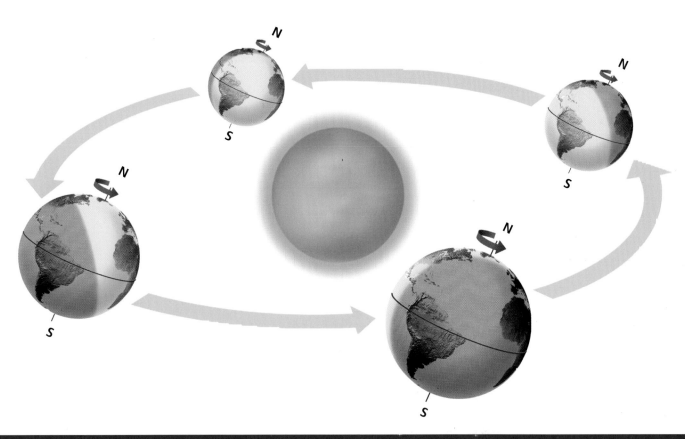

Radiation from the sun

The sun's energy is called radiation, which travels in "waves" of different lengths. Some of these waves form visible light that we can see. There are also shorter waves: gamma rays, ultraviolet light, and X rays. Infrared heat waves are longer, and radio waves are longer still. Visible light comes almost in between. This radiation is called the electromagnetic spectrum.

All radiation travels at 186,416 mi. (300,000 km) per second. This is the same as the speed of light.

▼ A rainbow is caused when the sun's light is split into its different colors by the rain. These are called the colors of the spectrum.

The Earth's invisible shield

The amount of radiation reaching the Earth is only one two-thousand-millionth part of the sun's output. The ozone layer in the atmosphere acts like an invisible shield stopping most of this radiation from reaching the Earth's surface. Ultraviolet and X rays would be very dangerous if they penetrated the atmosphere. Fortunately, visible wavelengths get through, bringing light to our unique planet.

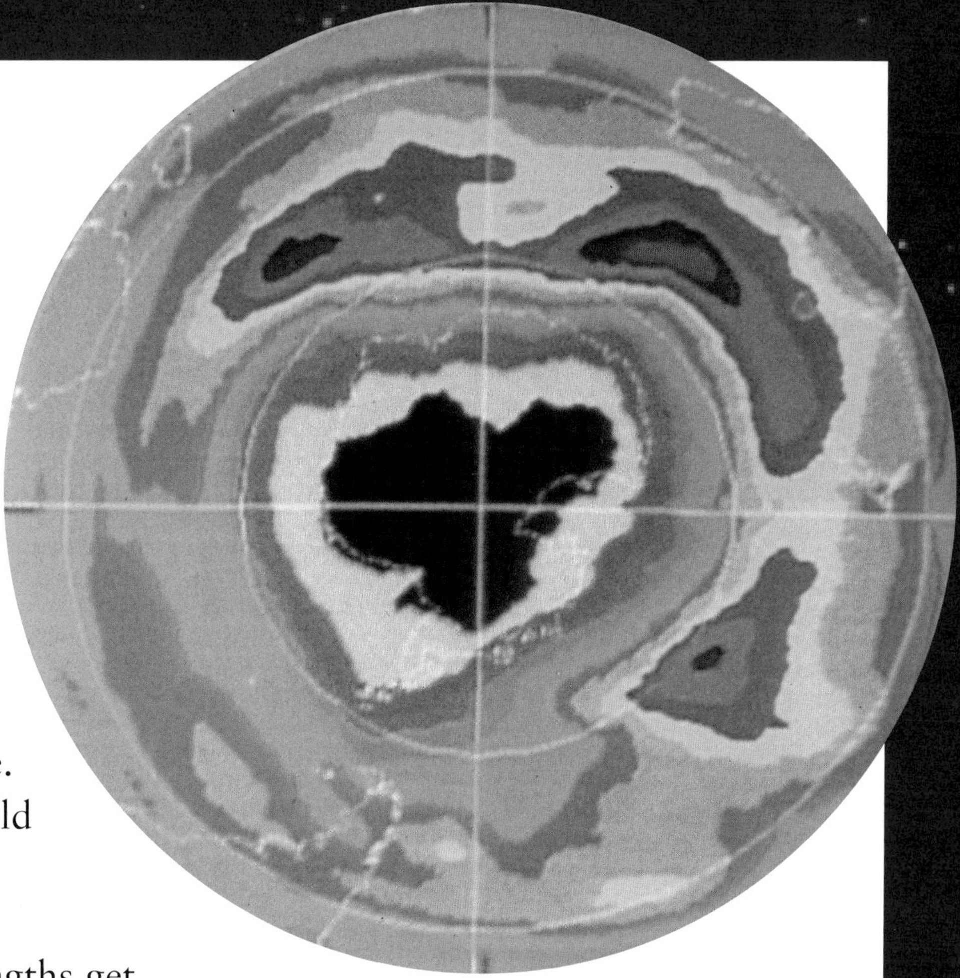

Holes in the ozone layer!

The ozone layer is slowly being damaged by pollution. Scientists are worried that "holes" in the ozone layer will let in more damaging radiation. The pollution is also causing carbon dioxide levels to increase in the atmosphere, creating the "greenhouse effect." Heat from the sun enters the atmosphere but cannot escape, causing our planet to warm up. Scientists are trying to figure out if the damage can be reversed.

▲ Satellites are able to keep watch on the development of holes in the ozone layer. One hole is shown here as the black patch in the center.

Radiation does not come just from the sun but from all over the universe.

Solar power

Radiation from the sun provides us with light and warmth, making the Earth a place where life can exist. The sun is free to us all. We don't have to pay for its light and heat.

We can also use the sun's power. The sun's energy can be converted into electricity using solar cells. Solar cells are used on satellites to provide electrical power. Thousands of small solar cells that look like tiny mirrors are assembled on panels attached to the satellite. These panels point at the sun and provide the

▲ Thousands of solar cells are assembled on panels attached to a satellite.

A typical communications satellite has two solar arrays like wings that span about 98 ft. (30 m) and generate 9 kilowatts of electricity.

power to make the spacecraft work. Solar cells have also been used to power aircraft and cars.

Most solar cells use a reflective material called silicon. But new materials such as gallium arsenide are now being used to provide even more electrical power, because they can attract more of the sun's energy.

Another way of getting power from the sun is called solar dynamics. Mirrors concentrate the sun's light to boil water to steam, which drives turbines. The turbines generate electricity.

Using the sun's energy to generate power is good for the environment, because it does not cause pollution in the atmosphere the way fuel-burning power plants do.

▼ Solar cells are also used to generate electricity for homes.

SOLAR ECLIPSES

The moon is much smaller than the sun. But it seems big to us because it is closer to the Earth. The moon sometimes passes in front of the sun, cutting out some or all of the sun's light. This is called an eclipse.

▲ During an annular eclipse, the outer rim of the sun can still be seen. Annular means "ring."

The longest possible duration of a solar eclipse is 7 minutes and 31 seconds. But the longest solar eclipse actually seen was only 7 minutes 8 seconds.

A total eclipse occurs when the moon passes across and covers the sun completely. This produces a deep shadow that reaches a small part of the Earth. Inside this shadow, an observer experiences one of the most dramatic sights anyone can see—the total eclipse. Outside this shadow, the moon cuts out only part of the sun. Because some of the sun can be seen, it does not become so dark. The observer sees a partial eclipse.

By flying an aircraft at a speed to keep up with the movement of the moon that creates the eclipse, some astronomers managed to experience a total eclipse lasting 72 minutes.

Another type of eclipse is called an annular eclipse. At its farthest point from the Earth, the moon looks slightly smaller as it passes in front of the sun. The outer rim of the sun can still be seen during this eclipse.

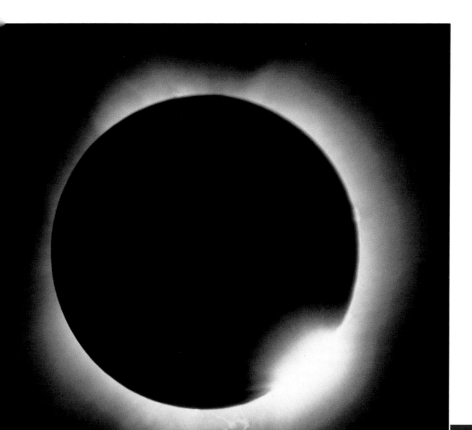

◄ A photograph of a total eclipse taken on July 11, 1991, in Mexico

SPACECRAFT EXPLORERS

If we flew too close to the sun, we would fry. No spacecraft has been able to get very close. Some unmanned spacecraft have been launched to observe the sun from a safe distance in orbit. Two *Helios* spacecraft were launched into solar orbit in 1975. They came within 30 million miles (48 million km) of the sun. The *Helios* probes survived temperatures hot enough to melt lead.

▼ *SOHO* took this image of the sun's surface, which shows that the sun is constantly changing.

The *Helios* probes reached a record speed of 408,762 mi (254,000 km) per hour.

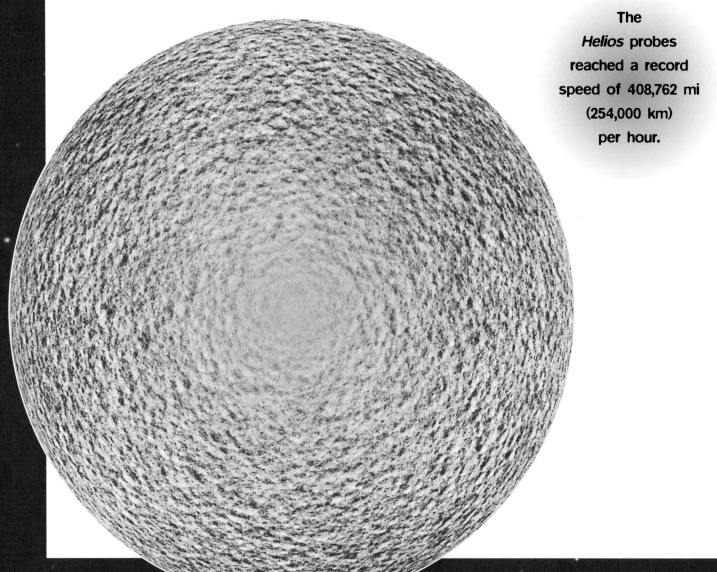

◀ *Ulysses* traveled at a speed of 32,115 mi. (51,682 km) per hour to escape the Earth's gravity to send it on its mission.

Many satellites in orbit around the Earth keep watch on the amount of radiation coming from the sun. Some satellites are used to warn the Earth about any strong bursts of radiation. These can affect the atmosphere and cause interference to radio transmissions.

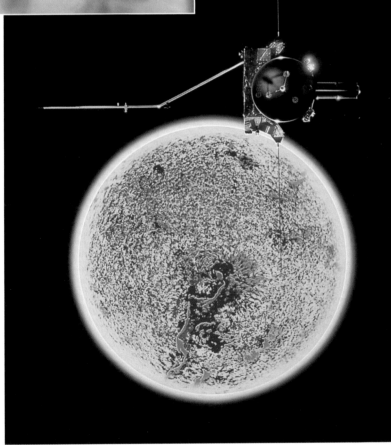

▲ The European *SOHO* keeps an eye continuously on the sun.

A European spacecraft called *SOHO*, the *Solar and Heliospheric Observatory*, was launched to study the sun in 1996. It was placed in a special orbit between the Earth and the sun. *SOHO* points at the sun all the time. It has sent back amazing images of the surface of the sun. Other pictures show solar flares and prominences. One spacecraft flew over the sun's poles in 1994–95. It was named *Ulysses*.

 # OBSERVING THE SUN

It is very dangerous to look directly at the sun! Never look at the sun through binoculars or a telescope. You will be immediately blinded by its heat and light!

The sun can only be safely observed by using a piece of white cardboard at the end of the telescope. The telescope then projects an image of the sun onto the cardboard. This must only be done under adult supervision. Point the telescope toward the sun. A cap must be placed over the eye lens. Hold the piece of cardboard several inches away from the end of the telescope. Take the cap off the lens. Move the telescope back and forth, and you will soon find that the sun's image is on the cardboard. Using this method, it may be possible to see sunspots as well.

The first observation of a sunspot was made in China, in 28 B.C.!

Most of the Kitt Peak telescope is underground. A cool, constant temperature ensures that the delicate scientific instruments work perfectly. ▶

Special telescopes and observatories have been built on the Earth to observe the sun. One of the most famous is at Kitt Peak, Arizona. This observes the sun in the same way that we can using an ordinary telescope. The image of the sun that the Kitt Peak observatory can project is much bigger. It allows astronomers to see the actual surface of the sun.

▲ The sun should be observed safely, like this.

NOTES FOR TEACHERS

Chapter 1 – The nearest star

Recreate a solar system in the classroom and imagine the outer limits outside. The Sun is a football. The Earth is 30 m away but Pluto is the seed of an apple 1.6 km away! Think of a landmark that is about that distance from the school.

Chapter 2 – The tiny sun

Refer to a simple star map and, if possible, arrange for the pupils to spot some of the most famous and brightest stars, to create the understanding of the vastness of the universe.

Chapter 3 – Sun facts

Create a simple but very high bar chart that shows dramatically the highest temperature on the Earth (58° C) and the hottest part of the sun (6,000° C).

Chapter 4 – The surface of the sun

The storms on the sun's surface can cause *aurora borealis*. Investigate further into this phenomenon finding out where and when it occurs and look at the patterns they create.

Chapter 5 – The sun and Earth

• Ask the pupils to look up at an object on the ceiling in front of them and walk forward to see the object "move" across the ceiling.

• Like a prism, a rainbow is a perfect demonstration of the visible light spectrum, showing its different colors. Ask the children to make up a rhyme to remember the different colors.

• Make a sundial. Start with a round base and place a pencil or stick vertically in the middle. At each hour of the day mark where the shadow lies on the base.

• Investigate buildings that have solar electricity generators or solar panels. There might be one near the school. Look at the different designs that are used and their advantages and disadvantages.

Chapter 6 – Solar eclipses

Demonstrate a solar eclipse using a lamp and a ball of the same size of the inside of the lampshade. The lampshade and bulb can be pointed at the pupils and the ball can be moved across its front.

Chapter 7 – Observing the Sun

• Ask a local astronomical society to arrange to demonstrate the safe way of observing the sun.

• Look on the Internet using the Web sites on page 31. There are regular updates on the sun's surface and a visual tour of the sun. Altogether a very safe way of observing our nearest star.

GLOSSARY

Astronomers People who study space.

Atoms The smallest possible parts of something.

Constellation A group of stars that we can see in the same area in the night sky. They may not be in the same galaxy.

Core The central part of something.

Equator The imaginary line around the middle of a planet or star, halfway between the polar regions.

Flares Sudden bursts of flame.

Galaxy A group of millions or billions of stars in the sky.

Helium A very light gas.

Hemisphere Half of a sphere. The equator divides the Earth into the Northern and the Southern hemispheres.

Hydrogen An invisible gas with no color or smell.

Nuclear Energy that is emitted from reactions involving atoms.

Observatory A place where astronomers study space, usually with powerful telescopes.

Orbit To go around.

Ozone layer A protective layer of gas in the Earth's stratosphere that absorbs harmful radiation from the sun.

Planet A solid, spherical mass in space that orbits a star.

Poles The northern and southern points of a planet or star that mark the axis of rotation.

Probes Unmanned spacecraft that transmit information about space back to Earth.

Radiation Various types of energy transmitted invisibly as electromagnetic waves.

Stars Large, glowing bodies in space made up of various gases.

Sunspots Dark spots that appear occasionally on the sun's surface.

Turbines A wheel-like device used for generating power.

Universe Everything that is in space.

FURTHER INFORMATION

Web sites:

sohowww.nascom.nasa.gov/ The Solar and Heliosheric Observatory. This site has the latest news on the sun direct from SOHO.

starchild.gsfc.nasa.gov/ Star Child: A Learning Center for Young Astronomers. This site is geared toward young people with an interest in astronomy.

Places to visit:

National Air and Space Museum
7th and Independence Ave., S.W.
Washington, D.C. 20560
(202) 357-2700
www.nasm.edu

NASA/Kennedy Space Center
Kennedy Space Center, FL 32899
(407) 452-2121
www.ksc.nasa.gov

BOOKS TO READ

Books to read:

Bevin, Finn. *Sacred Skies: The Facts and the Fables*. Children's Press, 1997.

Fowler, Allan. *Energy from the Sun*. Children's Press, 1997.

Gardner, Robert. *Science Project Ideas About the Sun*. Enslow Publishers, 1997.

Gilchrist, Cherry. *Sun-Day, Moon-Day: How the Week Was Made*. Barefoot, 1998.

Vogt, Gregory. *The Sun*. Millbrook Press, 1996.

Picture acknowledgments:

The publishers would like to thank the following for allowing us to reproduce their pictures in this book:
Bruce Coleman Ltd 2, 14, /Johnny Johnson *cover* [bottom], 13, /S. Nielsen 4, /Kim Taylor 16; Eye Ubiquitous /John Hulme 21; Genesis Photo Library *cover* [middle], *title page*, 19, 25 (bottom), /ESM 25, /NASDA, Japan 10; Popperfoto 18; Science Photo Library/J. Baum & N. Henbest 6, /Dr Fred Espenale 23, /David Hardy 12, /Ton Kinsberen *cover* [top], 25 (top), /NASA *contents page*, *cover* [main], 15, /David Parker 26, /Pekka Parviainen 8; Topham/Jerry Saxon 22; Wayland Picture Library/Telefocus 20.

The illustrations on pages 5, 7, 9, 11, 17 and 27 are by Peter Bull.

INDEX

All numbers in **bold** refer to pictures as well as text.